AMANDA GORMAN

Making a Difference with Her Words

By Katie Kawa

People Who Make a Difference

KidHaven PUBLISHING

Published in 2023 by
KidHaven Publishing, an Imprint of Greenhaven Publishing, LLC
29 E. 21st Street
New York, NY 10010

Designer: Deanna Paternostro
Editor: Katie Kawa

Photo credits: Cover Kathy Hutchins/Shutterstock.com; p. 5 AP Photo/Patrick Semansky, Pool; p. 7 Barry King/Alamy Stock Photo; p. 9 Oliver Contreras/Sipa USA/Sipa via AP Images; p. 11 WENN Rights Ltd/Alamy Stock Photo; p. 13 Alto Vintage Images/Alamy Stock Photo; pp. 15 (main), 18 Sipa USA/Alamy Stock Photo; p. 15 (inset) lev radin /Shutterstock.com; p. 17 dpa picture alliance/Alamy Stock Photo; p. 20 Everett Collection Inc/Alamy Stock Photo; p. 21 T.Sumaetho/Shutterstock.com.

Library of Congress Cataloging-in-Publication Data

Names: Kawa, Katie, author.
Title: Amanda gorman : making a difference with her words / Katie Kawa.
Description: New York : KidHaven Publishing, [2023] | Series: People who make a difference | Includes index.
Identifiers: LCCN 2021055789 | ISBN 9781534541627 (set) | ISBN 9781534541634 (library binding) | ISBN 9781534541610 (paperback) | ISBN 9781534541641 (ebook)
Subjects: LCSH: Gorman, Amanda, 1998–Juvenile literature. | African American women poets–Biography–Juvenile literature. | Poets, American–21st century–Biography–Juvenile literature. | LCGFT: Biographies.
Classification: LCC PS3607.O59774 Z72 2023 | DDC 811/.6 [B]–dc23/eng/20211104
LC record available at https://lccn.loc.gov/2021055789

Printed in the United States of America

CPSIA compliance information: Batch #CSKH23: For further information contact Greenhaven Publishing LLC, New York, New York at 1-844-317-7404.

Please visit our website, www.greenhavenpublishing.com. For a free color catalog of all our high-quality books, call toll free 1-844-317-7404 or fax 1-844-317-7405.

Find us on

CONTENTS

POETRY MAKES A DIFFERENCE

On January 20, 2021, Joe Biden officially became president of the United States. At his inauguration ceremony—the formal gathering marking the start of his presidency—many people shared **inspiring** words, including the new president himself.

One of the speakers that day was Amanda Gorman. She read a poem she'd written called "The Hill We Climb." The words Amanda wrote made many people feel hopeful and proud. They also called for change to make the United States a better and more united country. Amanda's words have inspired many people, and her story shows that writers can make a big difference in the world around them.

In Her Words

"So let us leave behind a country better than the one we were left."

— "The Hill We Climb"

Many people like to write poetry for fun or to get their feelings out. Amanda Gorman has also showed us that poetry can be used to call attention to problems in the world and to inspire people to work toward a better future.

THE PATH TO POETRY

Amanda Gorman's path to fame as a poet started when she was very young. She was born on March 7, 1998, and grew up in Los Angeles, California. She shares a birthday with her twin sister, Gabrielle. The two girls were raised by a single mother who's a teacher. Joan Wicks inspired her daughters to read, learn, and work hard.

Amanda loves books, and reading a lot as a kid made her want to write. She wrote short stories and then started writing poems. She learned that words have power and that she could use that power for good.

In Her Words

"Having a mom who is a teacher had a huge impact on me."

— Interview with the *Los Angeles Times* from January 2021

Amanda Gorman is a proud Californian, and many people in California are proud to say she's from their state. Shown here is a mural, or a large public painting, of her in Palm Springs, California.

FINDING HER VOICE

Over time, Amanda has become well known for reciting her poems, or saying them out loud. She's recited her poems on some of the biggest stages in the world, including President Biden's inauguration. She's also appeared on many television talk shows. However, speaking wasn't always easy for Amanda.

Amanda grew up with a speech disorder, which is a condition that makes it hard for someone to make the sounds they need to clearly speak to others. Amanda had a hard time making the sound of the letter *r*. She went to **therapy** and worked hard to become the strong speaker she is today.

In Her Words

"But I don't look at my disability as a weakness ... It's made me the **performer** that I am and the storyteller that I strive [try] to be."

— Interview with the *Los Angeles Times* from January 2021

President Joe Biden (shown here) also has a speech disorder. He grew up with a stutter. Both he and Amanda have shown people that a speech disorder doesn't have to stop someone from becoming a great public speaker.

BIG IDEAS AND HIGH HONORS

As Amanda kept working on her speaking skills, she also kept writing poetry. In 2014, she was named the Youth Poet Laureate of Los Angeles. A poet laureate is a poet honored for their skill and seen as a **representative** of the part of the world they come from. The next year, Amanda's first book of poetry came out. It was titled *The One for Whom Food Is Not Enough*.

Amanda's poems are often about big ideas and issues that are important to her. They often deal with what life is like for Black people, especially Black women, in the United States.

In Her Words

"I'm the daughter of Black writers who are **descended** from Freedom Fighters who broke their chains and changed the world. They call me."

— Interview with Michelle Obama for *TIME* magazine from February 2021

Amanda also founded an organization, or group, called One Pen One Page. It works to support young writers and to **encourage** young people to read.

A NATIONAL POET

In 2017, Amanda earned national attention when she was named the first National Youth Poet Laureate in U.S. history. In September of that year, she recited a poem she wrote, titled "In This Place (An American Lyric)," at the Library of Congress in Washington, D.C. It's the most important library in the United States! In this poem, Amanda celebrates, or honors, the **diversity** of the United States. However, she also calls attention to issues such as **racism** in this country.

Amanda continued to grow as a writer and an **activist** at school. After high school, she went to Harvard University in Boston, Massachusetts.

In Her Words

"There's a poem in Los Angeles
yawning wide as the Pacific tide
where a single mother **swelters**
in a windowless classroom, teaching
black and brown students in Watts
to spell out their thoughts
so her daughter might write
this poem for you."

— "In This Place
(An American Lyric)"

Amanda's words have opened doors for her to help others in many ways. She's even worked with the United Nations (UN), which is an organization that works for peace and human rights around the world.

WRITING FOR A DIVIDED COUNTRY

Amanda has many famous fans. One of those fans is Dr. Jill Biden, who's married to President Joe Biden. It was Jill who said Amanda would be a good choice to read a poem at her husband's inauguration ceremony.

Amanda made some big changes to her poem not long before she had to read it in front of the world. On January 6, 2021, people who were unhappy with Joe Biden being elected president attacked the U.S. Capitol in Washington, D.C. Many people were upset and afraid after this happened. Amanda knew she had to write about how divided the country had become.

In Her Words

"In everything you write, write something that is brave enough to be hopeful. In everything that you write, write something that is larger than yourself."

— Interview with Michelle Obama for *TIME* magazine from February 2021

January 6, 2021

Only two weeks before Amanda stood outside the U.S. Capitol to recite "The Hill We Climb," that same building was stormed by a large group of angry Americans—some of whom were **violent**.

INAUGURATION DAY

Before January 20, 2021, not many Americans knew Amanda Gorman's name. However, once she was done reciting "The Hill We Climb," she'd created a space for herself in American history.

Amanda's words spoke to a nation that was still struggling with the events of January 6. She said, "Somehow we weathered and witnessed a nation that isn't broken, but simply unfinished." Her poem addressed the divisions in the United States. However, it also called for Americans "to offer hope and laughter to ourselves." She wanted people to still feel hopeful, even in hard times.

In Her Words

"Let the globe, if nothing else, say this is true.
That even as we **grieved**, we grew.
That even as we hurt, we hoped.
That even as we tired, we tried."

— "The Hill We Climb"

Amanda was the youngest inauguration poet in U.S. history. She was only 22 years old when she recited "The Hill We Climb" at Joe Biden's inauguration. That day was also special for Amanda and other Black women across the country because it was when Kamala Harris became the first Black woman to become vice president of the United States.

IN THE SPOTLIGHT

Amanda's powerful words made her famous. In fact, those words were so powerful that they were collected into another book of poetry called *Call Us What We Carry*. Amanda also wrote a book for children called *Change Sings: A Children's Anthem*. Both books came out in 2021.

In addition to writing, Amanda has also continued her activism. For example, she works with an organization called 826 National, which helps students with their writing skills. Amanda has also used her voice to talk about racism, living with a speech disorder, and feminism—the belief that men and women are equal and should be treated as such.

In Her Words

"Poetry and language are often at the heartbeat of movements for change … Never underestimate the power of art as the language of the people."

— Interview with Michelle Obama for *TIME* magazine from February 2021

The Life of Amanda Gorman

1998
Amanda Gorman is born on March 7 in Los Angeles, California.

2014
Amanda is named Youth Poet Laureate of Los Angeles.

2015
Amanda's first book of poetry, *The One for Whom Food Is Not Enough*, comes out.

2017
Amanda is named National Youth Poet Laureate and recites "In This Place (An American Lyric)" at the Library of Congress in Washington, D.C.

2021
Amanda recites "The Hill We Climb" at the inauguration of President Joe Biden on January 20; recites a poem before Super Bowl LV on February 7; and has two books come out—*Change Sings: A Children's Anthem* and *Call Us What We Carry*.

Amanda's poetry has helped take her from classrooms in California to the U.S. Capitol—and even to the Super Bowl!

FROM POET TO PRESIDENT?

In February 2021, Amanda recited a poem she wrote, called "Chorus of the Captains," before Super Bowl LV—the biggest football game of the year in the United States. Her poem was written to honor frontline workers, such as health-care workers and teachers, during the **COVID-19 pandemic**. In addition to appearing before the Super Bowl, Amanda has been on many talk shows and magazine covers since she first recited "The Hill We Climb."

What's next for Amanda Gorman? She hopes to be president someday! She believes in the power of words to change the world, and her words are already making a big difference.

In Her Words

"For there is always light,
if only we're brave enough to see it.
If only we're brave enough to be it."

— "The Hill We Climb"

Be Like Amanda Gorman!

If you like sharing your thoughts and feelings through words or in other ways, such as by drawing or making music, practice doing that and sharing it with others.

Write your own poems about your life and causes that matter to you.

Help your younger siblings, cousins, or friends practice reading, especially if they have trouble with it.

Read books about many different kinds of people so you can learn their stories.

Write to government leaders about problems you see in the world around you and things you think need changing.

Amanda Gorman has shown people that you can make a big difference at a young age by using your words. Here are some ways you can follow in her footsteps!

GLOSSARY

activist: Someone who acts strongly in support of or against an issue.

COVID-19 pandemic: An event that began in China in 2019 in which a disease that causes breathing problems, a fever, and other health issues spread rapidly around the world and made millions of people sick in a short period of time.

descend: To come down from a source or person who lived long before you.

diversity: The quality or state of including many different kinds of people.

encourage: To make someone more likely to do something.

grieve: To feel or show very deep sadness, such as the sadness caused by the loss of a loved one.

inspiring: Moving someone to do something great.

performer: A person who uses a special skill to entertain an audience.

racism: The practice of treating others poorly because they are part of a different race, or group of people who look alike in certain ways. This word also relates to governments and societies that allow one race to be treated better than others.

representative: A person who stands or acts for others.

swelter: To be very hot and uncomfortable.

therapy: A method used to treat a mental or physical health problem.

violent: Relating to the use of bodily force to hurt others.

FOR MORE INFORMATION

WEBSITES

Amanda Gorman

www.theamandagorman.com

Amanda Gorman's official website has facts about her life and her writing, as well as links to her social media pages.

"Amanda Gorman Reads Inauguration Poem, 'The Hill We Climb'"

www.youtube.com/watch?v=LZ055ilIiN4

Visit YouTube to watch Amanda Gorman recite the poem that made her famous around the world.

BOOKS

Gorman, Amanda. *Change Sings: A Children's Anthem*. New York, NY: Viking Books for Young Readers, 2021.

Haynes, Danielle. *Inauguration Day*. New York, NY: PowerKids Press, 2020.

Minden, Cecilia, and Kate Roth. *Writing a Poem*. Ann Arbor, MI: Cherry Lake Publishing, 2019.

INDEX